Seven Car Loads of What You Need

Richard Stanton

Seven Car Loads of What You Need

Acknowledgements

Some of these poems have been previously published as follows:
'Tilba Tilba, New Year's Eve', 'Trackwork', 'Manly Maybe',
Quadrant, 2020
'Leaves in the Wire', *Quadrant*, 2019
'Waiting for Baby', *Mountain Secrets*, Ginninderra Press, 2019
'Cutting the Aniseed', *Imago*, 1997

Seven Car Loads of What You Need
ISBN 978 1 76041 973 8
Copyright © Richard Stanton 2020
Cover photo: Lorraine Stanton, Mungo Park
Author photo: Robert Wilson

First published 2020 by
Ginninderra Press
PO Box 3461 Port Adelaide 5015
www.ginninderrapress.com.au

Contents

Not Hannah's Town	9
Birthday	12
Tilba Tilba, New Year's Eve	13
Trackwork	15
Dementia	16
Eagle Canyon	18
Gillard's Beach Part 1	19
Gillard's Beach Part 2	23
Leaves in the Wire	24
Waiting for Baby	25
Manly Maybe	26
A Range of Blue Hills	27
Watching a Loaded Mousetrap	29
Pelicans on the Darling	30
Alexander Street	31
Wolgan Valley Recall	32
Truck Driver	33
Thunder Across the Atlantic	34
Blue Lake Sequence	39
Burning Dogs	42
Towards Evening	43
Constructed Dignity	45
The Plan	46
Cutting the Aniseed	47
Do You Love Me?	48
Drawn Over the Bar	49
Gardner's Inn	50
Hay Plain	51
High Country	52
Hong Kong	53

Kerouac's Cradle	54
Leavings II	56
An Oxford Street Café	57
Mercury Bird	58
Against the Odds	59
New Year	63
Oceans and Lines	67
Out the Window 12.9.80	68
Balranald	69
Seems Darker	70
Paterson's Curse	74
Red-haired Girl	75
Ringmaster	79
Rising Tide of Laughter	80
Silent Water Fall	81
Cessnock	82
Sparrows	83
Summer Solstice	84
Sunday	85
Termination Overrun	86
The Desert	87
The Hand of the Carver	88
Cracking Plaster	89
Young Tom	90
Too Many Fruit Shops	93
Torment	94
Days to Play	96
Vivus Sectio	97
When the Flagon Was Finally Empty	99
Whites of Their Eyes	100
Windbreak	101
West Wyalong: A Postmodern Impression of the Bush	102

City Dream Country Nightmare	104
Another Sunrise	105
Arc of an Angel	106
Axeman's Interior Monologue	107
Backroad	111
Dog's Dinner	112
Dr Wisdom's White Hot Hall of Adrenalin	113
Feathers	115
Dubbo Abattoir	116
Glassy Mountain Lake	118
Illusory Fantasy	120
Kite Day #1	122
Kite Day #2	123
Passing Replay	124
Wendy	126
Mittagong Morning	127

Not Hannah's Town

The town
Now
A cleft palette
Bifurcated
Halved if you like
Matt white one side
Black gloss the other
Where Hannah More's
Imaginings
Have been redacted to dust

Old ways fail
To hold
As the centre
Cannot

Slowly they come at first
Dribbling in
A couple here
A single there
Incrementally too at first
The architecture
A new storey here
A knockdown up there
Buoyed by Collins Street
Or Pitt
Take your pick

Whispered threats
From old timers
About raising the wall
Will do nothing to stop the flood
Sentient
Before the fall
As institutions
Long the preserve
Of
Tom Hod
Jack Anvil
(CWA Country Club Bowlo Art Society)

Need new blood
Transfused
From somewhere else
They said
To each other
At the whine bar
As they did the numbers
As the pub itself
Rose and Crown no less
Succumbed
To a hipster makeover
Virtue signalling its facebook self
By evicting stinking sexist racist fishos
From the front bar
Easy done
Pull down the front bar
Too easy

Now all the city kiddies
Feel safe while
Mummy and Daddy selfie through
Tempered glass
Backs to the bay
Momentarily

No truth + no belief = no faith

Birthday

Why do we not buy ourselves
birthday presents?
So many brave expectations
deflated
by texts
phone calls
nothing truly tangible
other than a book, or two.

Les Murray's greatness
though
is no substitute
for a metallic blue 911.

Tilba Tilba, New Year's Eve

Six hours south they drive
pioneers of the east
sustained
in the early evening drizzle
by blood-orange Cointreau
on ice
tweets
selfies

Set strategically
about the iron fire cauldron
as the Possum's Cloak descends

Sparks fly
droplets fall
settling quietly on
rockabilly outfits
expensive and uniform
complete with
ironic hats

Go gently observing
Bondi hipsters accessorising
in particular with cigarettes slim
lest they forget their manners
point fingers
call you
bear
curiously named Judgy Wudgy

Within hours of the sparkler-adorned
switch of years
weary
of the Game of Country
in convoy
Snapchat to hand
they motor north

Renewed by ironic looks
that will become legend
when once again they
are embedded in the east

Far, far from the descent of the Possum's Cloak
raging against the dying of the light

(With grateful acknowledgements to John Beresford Kingsmill and Dylan Thomas)

Trackwork

I could always hear the sound
of the long-distance train
from my bedroom window
even though
I was more than a mile and a half from its nearest track

The warm evening breeze
caught the travelling bogies
flinging their faraway sounds
right into my childhood
leaving lingering the smell of somewhere better

Dementia

Talked to Tom Hallahan's son
the other day
on the phone
asked how he was
Now
in hospital with dementia
getting worse

He spends his nights
trying to find
escape routes
but he can't come home
just yet
too far gone
needs constant care

Had to take the
rifle bolt
out of the safe
Will leave it out at my place
with his car keys

Found the ammo
in the desk drawer.
In my glovebox
now
until I get back out to my place
hide it all out there

He won't be coming out there
again though
too far gone

Next week they say
he might go home
to his place
after the ACAT

Will need constant
round the clock
care
someone has to stay
at night

He fell out of bed
out at the farm
I thought it was
a fucking roo
got in at the back veranda

It was Dad
crying out
banging on the wall

Lucky
he would have
perished from the cold.

Eagle Canyon

Right up in the canyon
where the river takes
a sweeping great turn
before it reaches the dam

An eagle flew across the sun
and flooded our canoe with its wingspan

Gillard's Beach Part 1

The sea looks calm after your run
calm enough to plunge
into
feel the warmth
relative
of nineteen-degree winter waves

Beyond, though, where you could not see
five knots of current running south
faster than you could swim in your lycra bike gear
after a hot beach run

Your clothes
personal effects (they call them)
waiting on the sand
to be discovered three hours after
fourteen-thirty when you went in intending
surely to be out within fifteen minutes
but no
three hours later your effects
discovered
with no trace

Alarms raised
by nineteen-hundred.
Eden water police
Whisky Papa Two Four on scene begins
a long-leg search pattern
between Tathra and Bithrey's Inlet
without success
and a workplace requirement
for downtime

As crew begin operational
risk assessment on
BG30 before 0540hrs
in the dark ready to proceed to LKP

But wait says marine area command
wait until light no sense in provoking extra risk

So wait the crew does
then drives south through three metre swell
plotting set and drift
plotting search pattern
linking with MB30, WP24
becoming on-scene controller

In one mile standoff
observers port and starboard between vessels
twelve knots bearing zero one five True
turning ninety through ninety
repeating pattern
in a twelve-hour day
before refuelling finding beds

Then again the following day
back to the sea
SES on land checking all beach tracks
four-wheel drive roads
may have been carried south
emerged and be injured
somewhere in the bush

helo and drone
hovering without success
RIBS darting
into all possible coves and crevasses
divers under rock shelves

But no.
Success is elusive
there is no sign
other than remnants of die-marking
as the sea calms
wind drops
by the third day
there is not much hope
as the
search and rescue
turns to
search and recovery
turns to
search and despair

Forty-eight hours
boats stood down
return to their pens
crews stood down
return to their homes
washed down
refuelled

Ready for the next time
a runner
takes to the water
becomes to the news media
a swimmer
becomes to the coroner
a lost soul.

Gillard's Beach Part 2

But wait you say
There is no swimmer
There is no runner
There is no twin brother
There is only
A hoaxer
After three days of running
With the fabrication
You disappear
Into the ether
Rather than the ocean
For the police to pursue
Only this time the
Pursuit will not be
One of rescue
But
One of detention
For your manufactured
Disappearance of your twin brother
Leaving behind
A million dollars' worth
Of search and rescue
Where the operational
Is praised
Bitterness prevails.

Leaves in the Wire

My mind today is wire
Strung between pale weather-ravaged fence posts

Hordes of yellow leaves
Congregate and scuffle against my soft-soled feet

With the smell of winter
On the wind I wait impatiently for a southerly

To free my bottom strands

Waiting for Baby

I've done this waiting before, on a mountain
Ten thousand feet, despairing
For that vital break in the weather
Rolling cigarettes making another brew
Reading Emily Dickinson rucksack packed
Retying prusik loops, adjusting crampon straps
In a smoky festering hut
Until ten days later the hogsbacks break a moment after midnight
Out and up, headlamps umbilical rope, first slot opens
Between rock and ice, belays over snowbridge
Last two hundred only pain no strength remains in arms legs
Cramps
Summit
Before dawn

Sack packed again, waiting
Reading Emily Dickinson after all these years
No cigarettes, making a brew only a few days to go
Hold on for a break in the weather
Another brew in a clean warm house
Until ten days later the waters break, monitor's out, heartbeat's up
Last two hundred only pain some strength remains in arms legs
Contractions
Birth
Before dawn

Manly Maybe

Smells of chicken
Pizza shops and fish
Maybe
Eat them
In the sun
Warm wine with a paper dish

And the girls

Ruining their feet
In rubber thongs
But
Not my eyes
With their breasts
And
See-through sarongs.

A Range of Blue Hills

I invested unwisely
if my school reports
are to be believed
my formative years
wedged between a lazy river
and a range of blue hills.
Carmarthen adventures
coupled with a suicidal grandfather
provoked the end of family history

Until now
when a bit of spadework
unearths
from Birdseye Corner
a Great x 3
sharpening axes and road building implements for
William Cox
as he drives towards
Lachlan Macquarie's
goal of a buggy pass
hewn into yellow sandstone
basalt-capped

'Ironbark' Cox wrote
'Hard as nails'
bending metal
So 'back to Field's for repairs'

Grind out a way across ridges
between valleys
named in honour of
John Jamison
Francis Grose
William Pitt
George Caley

Named unwisely in history
if woke virtue signallers
are to be believed.

Watching a Loaded Mousetrap

I'm waiting for you
You little grey rodent
To stick your head
Out of the black space
Behind my stove
And into my loaded mousetrap

Watching for your
Darting pink nose
When it sniffs my
Tantalising yellow cheese
Resting idly on the arm of death.

Pelicans on the Darling

Pelicans
Scattered across
The brown smoothness
Of the Darling
On each reach
Each bend

Paddling aside only
When the big steamer
Travelling six knots
Corners as if on a
Slalom

Pelicans
The markers
Brown water matching
Brown banks reaching
Out to brown trees
In the early morning
Yellow light.

Alexander Street

The little house up on Alexander Street
had a quality all its own.
The little house up on Alexander Street
would not have had such a quality
if the most beautiful girl
in the world
hadn't lived there.

Sometimes she was so pretty
she forgot there was a lemon tree
in the backyard
and went shopping for lemons.

Wolgan Valley Recall

Sat amongst wild roses
We did
That day
In the rain
With the oil shale
Mines
In ruined non-work
Around us
Until the night
Curling like
Smoke
Tilled the sky.

Truck Driver

Once a truck driver
and I
threw oranges at a telegraph pole.
He hit the pole twice
I missed every time.
The pole was
a long way out of reach
I was only ten years old
Anyway.

Thunder Across the Atlantic

You quietly crept up on me
Layering your thoughts
Like fingers of foam
Upon my sand mine(d)
Until
Like a headlight mesmerised macropod
Your being
My nothingness
Was all I could hear
Below the roar of thunder
As you crashed into me
Crushed what I had
Until then
Believed to be sensibility

Gravitationless now I
Aim-less-ness-ly
Want you
Here as I write you
Instead
Not even in another life
Can I imagine we will
You know
The f word
Despite litcrit pretensions

'Stronger than you'
Jane said
Against the barn
On a warm-breeze autumn night
'Mentally'

Long ago
Seems
But it was fewer than seven years
And now I want desperately
To write you
Baring to your gardenia beauty
The true soul of the poet
For your decision.

What a path
No map
No route description
But yes! You say
There it is laid out for you
Aristotelian
No need of roping
Put away those crampons
Steps have been cut
Wide and deep in shadow
But wait again
There is a further choice…
Off to the side…
A sharper edge…
You failed to attempt
Though I can see your initials
Carved in the base of the rock
My beauty
And your gardenia fragrance
Lingers long among the strewn
Shards of windswept

Stones
At the base of the face –
Is this where you want me to go?

Unending signifiers
Have stolen you
Replaced parts
Returned a counterfeit
'And what a delight'
You though bare I want
«*Avec tout la vérité*»
Capable of salvage
From within the reverse cycle of
Postmodernist playfulness
Now comes the hard part.
I am falling in love with you
I want to stop…
I want to get off here…
I want to unrope…
«Last signifier»
«Express to full circle»
«Three hours to Plato»
«Aristotle for breakfast»
Then all stops to Derrida « « «
But I want to get off
Yeah nah
I want to
Pursue
Higher
Deeper

I want it all and
Bugger the cost
– Cost?

There's always that
Waiting with
Manicured nails
No Red
And where did the time go?
How did we get there?
I don't remember walking
Floating maybe
Trolley-filled margaritas

Now everything has changed
There's no going back
It has all been acted through
To an ovation beyond recall
And I am drained
Not since seventies acid
Has the explosion of colour
Gardenia-induced
Torn back the chapters and
Spread life across it with such uncommon
Finality.

God. I'm fucked.
And you, my gardenia beauty
Are the Fuck-ault
Now a few more lines (20 precisely)
Then I can screw

Back in the drain plug
If it's not stripped
Wiping first away fragments
Of brain, lungs
Is that heartblood
Puddling merrily
Around my toes?
Maybe I am already too late
Saving only the final signifier
In case construction is someday
Delivered
As the link
In the circle
To join Aristotle's fingers at some point
Seamlessly
Then you and I
Can begin again
(Not enough lines)?
It'll do.

Blue Lake Sequence

Light on water
Lake and fall
Moon and sun
Watch them all

Silhouette of
Rough wool cloth
Against the night
Against the frost

2. Copperheads Return to the Snow

What your word's worth
In an alpine meadow silence
Through buttongrass
Meandering with the wildness
And Twynam dwarfing the dividing range.

3. Saturday Arvo

In the afternoon on Carruther's Peak
I soak the 4 o'clock sun
While you
Wake somewhere in France

It will shine on you
While I prepare for the night
In the closeness of darkness
Death
Is no nearer

4. Blue Lake

I watched the moon rise over Blue Lake
Felt the meaning of death
There in the night
In the closeness
More understanding
Came over that moraine wall
On the edge of space

5. Early

Waking to pink on Townshend
Tea
Then climbing again
Sunday
Stretching southward
More tea
Reaching the end
As the sun pushes over the saddle

6. Sunday Afternoon

These mountains
So quiet
Except the Good Doctor
Breathing
Lying stretched on warm granite

Low cloud drifting lazily
In from Lady Northcote's

There is no other sound
Here on Mueller's Peak
Sunday afternoon

7. Still Sunday Afternoon

The scratching pencil
Buzzing blowfly
And wind fluting not in chimneys
But through
Fissures in the weathered rock
Extend the silence further

8. Cootapatamba

In the tent
In the night
All five
Wait for the snow

3 o'clock maybe
It's right
Noises of tea
Sipping

Sniffing
Against the cold
Unlacing of boots
Catching clips
In the sound of sleeping bags.

Burning Dogs

Across the street
Inside a warm winter's morning
Backroom
Of the pet hospital
There are no sounds
Of barking

A column of smoke
Filtering
From an unobtrusive pipe
On the roof
Is testimony
To Friday's burning's

As ash floats down
To rest with finality
On cars
In Crow's Nest's rooftop parking.

Towards Evening

You took him with you
driving north
as the sun descended
along the New England

Twenty-four he was again
remained

Long lines of hills
where you spilled
flagons of cheap wine
over youth with no change

Was he twenty-four again
or will he always be
if listening to Neil Young
is a sign

Still the descending sun
down the sharpening gradient
assists the doors of perception
to open once more
a crack
fleetingly framed
with the backdrop of evening

Tell him the lemons will never ripen
tell him there will never be enough time
advise him now, right now as you run north
while reality travels stretched
south

Tell him there is a longer season
to listen
as frogs
cattle
hooves of the newborn loper
distill in the outside air.

Constructed Dignity

These Sunday morning
streets
are working the same
appalling silences on me
as I remember childhood
Sunday afternoons
on the back veranda
of my grandmother's
decayed existence
living with the constructed
dignity
a suicidal husband provides
instead of life.

The Plan

On the stairs
On departure
You wanted to kiss her
Instead
You she smiled obliquely
When the real plan
In your head
Said
Don't leave
The afternoon is too young
Unendingly bold
With the scent of your gardenia beauty
Then you she
Gone
Around a concrete corner

Only the gardenia beauty
Remained
Embedded leaded
In your mind
Where it began
Where it may end
Where it became
An unbroken wave
Pierced by its own less than profound
Structuralist utility
There was really
No choice.

Cutting the Aniseed

Only powerful blows from the hand
Holding a sharpened scythe
Will take out month-old growth
As the aniseed tumbles broken to the deck

No use trying to put the mower through
Only conk out as it hits the hard base
Though it was alright for smaller tufts
Still wet and pungent
With leftover frost endings on cold winter afternoons

Down the side of the riverbank it grew
Solidly for a couple of slow generations
Until road-widening, tourists
Pushed it forever under a bank of geotextiles

The smell was still the same though
Near Balmain power station driving along Victoria Road
It poured in the wound-down window
As a whippersnipper in vain
Slashed and slashed with breaking cord

Needs a sharpened scythe in a powerful hand
To knock back the big base growth, mate.
Smells just the same
Quality control hasn't changed in fifty years.

Do You Love Me?

I had a girlfriend
When I was 3
Did you kiss her?
Bet you did.
We poked fun
At a next-door spaniel
From the top
Of a wonky paling fence
I fell
Cracked my head
More fearful of the dog than
Tasting my 3-year-old
Blood
Draining from my noggin.
Is that
What happened?

Drawn Over the Bar

The best way
To cut it fine
Is to
Buy a ticket
In a chook raffle
Ten minutes
Before the ferry
Is due to leave

Part 2

Caught the ferry

Gardner's Inn

Jesus you're right
and it is a good feeling
not just the beer or the night
it's you
and smiles
and hands
and will you
live with me
that's right
here's a lifetime
in the mountains
serenity
out of sight.

Hay Plain

Crossing the Hay Plain at
one hundred and
fifty-five
the Nam vet
riding to Adelaide
on the Harley with
the mate
just out in front.
Headlights
beam on in to
Mallee blackness
as an old owl
calls across a
once mighty Murray
anabranch
downstream in the
darkness.
As the television
funeral of a sad lost
girl proceeds along
a sunlit London street.

High Country

Through the contrast
Of light
Intermittent cloud
On every peak

A saddle
Joins
In umbilical wonder
Separating crystal creeks

With granite outcrops
Tilting sideways
Against such force

Contemplate the movement
As a drawstring
Closes off
An empty purse

Or moss
Growing on the lee side
Of the
Wind and rain

Dying with the snow
Until spring
Gives silent birth again.

Hong Kong

When the bag
Of squirming brown frogs
Is empty
Its contents
Neatly divided
Sliced and chopped
Only the image remains
Along with some dried blood
Ground into
A narrow strip of macadam
Between market stalls
Heavy and humid
With the duckshit smell
Of unidentifiable body pieces.

Kerouac's Cradle

Cradle Mountain
Is a nice mountain
It's not so big
But it's very friendly

Hardly anyone
Ever
Dies on its slopes

Cradle Mountain
Is very sympathetic
Towards people
Crawling about on its sides

Not like some mountains
That get upset
At the first sign of a crawl

Jack Kerouac wrote
A whole book
Accounting for a winter
He spent on a mountain

That's a lot of time
To write about
A mountain

I don't think Cradle Mountain
Will get that much
Of any
Dharma

Oddly enough
That book never did find its way
Back to me.

Leavings II

And I talk of death
With you
As if it were hard by
Discover a source
A dialogic
Fecund with a framework for existence
Laid bare
On the deadly stone ground of the past

An Oxford Street Café

Tuesday 31 January 1978

Can't write
Feeling bright
Café black
And I've got all night

Excess verse
Quaintly terse
Marble table
And my empty purse

Going home
Not quite alone
Feeling fine
And I'm on my own.

Mercury Bird

Blue room poster bed
Boots and hat deep red

Blue room over head
Witching dreams blood red

Blue room fear and dread
Incense thick burning red

Blue room wrong words said
Axis shifts heart stops dead

Mercury bird tilts *axis mundi*
Mercury bird come back to me

Against the Odds

Your old house
Dug down one storey
Below the hill to
Withstand blows
From the prevailing 40-knot nor'easter
Spigots undrilled, undressed
Stacked against the garage wall
Yet to be screwed to
New veranda railing
Half painted in blue undercoat

Sad tomato plants
Rotting among mounds
Of cow manure left untended
While you lie in bed
Waiting to battle belligerent
Nurses
Keen to keep you off the grog
On your meds
Daily
Until you can stand by yourself
Again
Without the walking chair
With four front wheels that
Won't push past the
Smallest clump of kike

Blue rope pink now from
Blistering sun
Dangles swinging in

The wind the only sign
Of movement other than
Dead kike
Shifting from under the wheels
Of your rusted ute
Tray out to the sea
Spray penetrating body
Cavities after three months
Standing waiting to be
Driven
Up and down the grassy bank
To keep the battery
Alive

Lying there half dead
Yourself
But still intent on
Revving up the other
Passengers, customers, patients
More sick than you
You said when you got
Back
Sitting in front of the TV
With a light beer
Because that won't
Hurt me medication
I've got a box of the stuff
But jeez I'm
Pleased to be off that
Bloody cortisone

Today, though, is brighter
The sound of the sea
Roars up on the nor'easter
Greeted by spigots
Screwed in measured spaces
Almost done
As you in your familiar flanno
And blue school cap
(No hat no play)
Supervise a lumbering mate
Who started screwing early
First cutting each piece
Individually
Both of you supervised
By a
Block of a woman
Burnt black by too much sun
Shaved head
Without talking
Speaking, measures the level of satisfaction

While downstairs
Discarding a guitar for a paintbrush
Your paraplegic son
Dabs at a piece of lattice
With what's left of undercoat
His girlfriend
Herself a grandmother
Cooks dinner for five
In an electric frypan

(No stove downstairs)
And the next-door neighbour
In puttees, Akubra and shorts
Same age as you
Rakes and rakes
Among the fallen foliage
Disturbing three months stillness
On the lee side
As you
Still shaky
But smiling
Staccato back and forth
Measuring the workmanship
Adjusting in your mind
As the first grin of the
Season
Cracks you ancient
Now less-weathered face
Your house
Smiles in return.

New Year

Towards midnight
I close cigar clips
Empty ashtrays
As next door
Legal Capital Territory
Fireworks
Explode across the river
On this New Year's Eve
Where loud radios
Speed boat motors roar
In the still evening air
As neighbours display
Masculinity
Until childlike
Those under twelve
Retreat to bed
Before the sun arcs over the river
Over the last line of eucalypts
Over the horizon
And Arthur,
Animated
Earlier, on my side of the river
Sold twelve pallets
He said
As I walk home in hot afternoon
Calculating
That's a lot of beer
That the blow-ins might consume
Before tomorrow
Before they convoy
Out

Trailing half-used boats
Because
Foul weather closed up all but the last few days
Of the two weeks annual

In groups of houses up and down the street now
Lights blaze with end-of-year groupings
While in between
Old David
And his kind
Sit alone with only the tide
As evidence
Of the change
Each morning

As we wait in groups
Alone
Drinking talking acting waiting
In Paris
Booksellers pull up shutters
Streets weep to slough off
New fallen snow
Still more than a
Day and a half away from
Our celebratory anticipation

The bread shops there don't close at midday
Having sold the full production run
Thin lipped and pleased
That tourists
Might miss their daily loaf

Not half as pleased as Arthur
To have a full house
Until tomorrow
When they convoy north and south
There is no east
Without a boat and bait.

As the burning sun cuts a finite arc
Low
Sinking on today
In Bermagui
Over Paris
Its brightness is hours away
Yet incidental
As Parisians wake
Muffling scarves and gloves
Against snowflakes
Briskly seek out
Celebration cakes
Galettes
Over and over
Endless crowns
Joyous with small ceramic treats
Deep inside
As overcast clings to the upturned
Booksellers shutters
As fireworks for one moment
Jamboree over the Bermagui River

While the deaf dog,
Oblivious to candles, champagne corks
Thoughts of snow-covered railings
Along the Seine
Snores on and on
Contoured within the futon
Dreaming of tomorrow's walk
Along a very different river.

Oceans and Lines

Can you see
There is a trade wind

Out beyond the tide
Out beyond horizon

Out beyond your vision
If it has yet begun

Out the Window 12.9.80

Clouds on glass
Flat-bottoming
Across the airways

White to grey pass
Speeding on
Like a freeway

No kamikazes
In that lot.

Balranald

Stopped for pies
in Balranald
on a Friday arvo
in spring
we did.

Once on the way.
Again
on the way back

And the black Levi's shirt
on a rack
outside the haberdasher's
at $50
was such a find
it fitted.

With
Howard's change
in the TCF
tariff policy
the tag inside that
reads China
may
one day soon come home.

Seems Darker

Seems darker in winter you sum
as night sky toys with the beginning of a moon
full, sensuous with waxing
watchful of emerging ice crystals

Never shone before though you say into this room
white in the winter night while a blaze of sawn timber
creates warmth fills the rooms

Lying on the floor watching you watch the sky
childhood dreams awaken in me the adult
less tenor than a once proposed journey
to the Cordillera Blanca
in pursuit of jagged rock and ice

Glimpsing the realisation that not yet
am I imprisoned by externalities
taking aim is far less easy through a wonky sight
as you ponder the darkening sky in its winter mantle

'I saw some cats this morning' I say
trying to entice you away from your moon
'In the river near the bank
Bloated, bellies up floating waiting with
Stiff legs to catch a limb and hold
Thanklessly their puffy sacks lifeless
Before floating further towards and over
The weir into heavenlessness'

You leave the curtain then to fall back
of its own accord
turning to watch the flames in a moonless backdrop

'Following the mother still defenceless they were
Even blind before the birth of death of life ending'

Watching you watch the fire streaming up the flue
reactionless to the lifeless description of floating
cats' bodies

'You know mainly it is white intense I mean
The light in summer' you respond
'After Christmas that helps on such sticky afternoons
To make choices of pieces
He is using colour tentatively now, the potter'

Unsure but not needing to let such meaning escape meaning
as must have been so obvious to you
the question I framed made no impression on your monologue

'We travelled some way by any standard
To stand holding adoring what some suggest is created
By a man who owns a church but has no religion
Then driving home not a wind but a breeze
Following up with us as the coastline
Furtively winding'

With nothing more than listening as an available option
I do and you tell me
'Screaming over water southerly disrupting
A glass crystal surface'

An event I had not shared nor wanted

after such a description to really be part of
but like my cat story it had to have more than
such a false ending that you went on to describe

'Dropped what he said later had been
The same mixture of colour as my eyes
And I think that's really why he liked it
And I got it and we did say like too often
But was that colour part of the idea he began with?'

'But it smashed because I tried to close out buggers
Taking up the space I needed for him'

Then I realised you were telling me of long gone love
that I had known of and waited very occasionally
for you to delve into
on such winter long nights as this

'Buggers taking up space
I wanted to bang heads in compensation
No the four dollars did not matter
It could have been four million
Only I did it without control'

That helps a lot you know
but I didn't whether it helped in banging heads
or understanding buggers corroboreeing on the lawn

No matter
you will tell me more
someday
and the picture I have will need no more explanation
smiling at the fire.

Paterson's Curse

Right outside the
Banjo Paterson bar
I got a
Flat tyre
All the way from Walgett
Must be a night
To beat all nights

Red-haired Girl

Through your front window
As you sit waiting
You see a girl walking along the road

In the road
Slowly

Sometimes stopping
To wait for another girl
Around the same age
Never to catch up
Only to make sure she still follows

The girl you see first has beautiful red hair
She pauses to wait
For the other girl

Your red-haired girl
Wears fashionable beige shorts
With a white blouse and sandals

She leads grudgingly
The other girl with black socks and sandals
A skirt too long for the day's hot morning
Although now
Late in the afternoon
There is the longest hint of storm
Rising over the angophoras
As they peel gently away their layers
Of grey winter
To reveal
Grave orange beauty

As she waits for the other girl she turns
Watching her approaching foot flap
As each black shoe
Tries vainly to track the path
Of the first step

Alas your red-haired girl
Is soon lost from view
And now you can see what has always been there
A chair
One angophora
The veranda
Quiet pots of exhausted late spring bulbs
A deckchair
A green watering can
It will rain shortly

The girl with the red hair has gone
She was carrying a great deal
On her shoulders
In her mind
Slowly, resolutely the other girl followed
Attached by an invisible chain
Unable to follow smoothly
The path that was being laid evenly
Someone else's mind
Someone else's function
Someone else's form

Two deckchairs
The second blending
In to a reflection off the window
With its eight glass panels
Open
Sifting

The girl with the red hair inspired you
But she's stuffed
Really
Traipsing her halfwit sister around
On an invisible chain

The red-haired girl flies
Brave spirited
Through the indignity of it all
With her hair tied
In a tight knot
On top of her head

Long gone now
Somewhere down the road
Got off the road and on to the grass path
As she went out of sight
With the other girl

You want her to come back
And tell you
If you were right in your assumptions
Tell you the truth
Not a small amount of it
If truth comes in amounts
Or degrees
Or volume
Mass sequence
A sequence of truth
Where would that lead

We all follow the path of the red-haired girl
She's leading us all, she knows the truth.

Ringmaster

Close your caravan door
Ringmaster
After such a splendid performance

Your destiny
Is inalienable

Your matinee accolades
May have died away
Minutes earlier
On such a damp
Wind swept
Moral middle-class afternoon

Though at least
Very least
Your destiny
Remains

Ringmaster
Close your caravan door
On the simple moral middle class
Confusion
Alleviated
This wet Sunday afternoon
By trapeze.

Rising Tide of Laughter

Sometimes when I'm away
life drifts slowly on
getting back together
makes it seem so long

Every day formalities
leave you on a tide
a rising tide of laughter
even when you cried

There's so much more to do
the meaning in your eyes still says
I'm very very wise

Plant a spark of reason
turn it into doubt
drift across the desert
never talk it out

When every word's been written
and every song's been sung
I'll think about my life with you
and maybe come undone

There's so much more to do
the meaning in your eyes still says
I'm never very wise

Take me for your lover
always be my friend
keep your eyes wide open
never let it end.

Silent Water Fall

The streets are alive
hollow with the sound
of silent water fall

Monday morning urgency
of sirens screaming
yesterday seems small

Blue forest filled
with green and streaming water
tumbling down black cliffs

Monday morning filled
with steel-grey walls
of 32nd floor bleak lifts

Slippery with green moss
and silent
with the sound of water fall

Cessnock

Often it rains so hard in Cessnock
It's truly a wonder
Little arks don't sprout up
In what's left of the cornfields

Is it going to rain now
Or are the sparrows
Hiding under the eaves
Of a false alarm

Perhaps the sparrows
Won't get any bread at all
Tomorrow
If they go on behaving like this.

Sparrows

The sparrows are singing again today
As they fly for the bread
Tossed out on the lawn

Today won't be so easy
Though the sun might be shining,
The air might be autumn warm,

The bread
Still has the crust on
And is getting harder as the day gets longer.

Summer Solstice

The days
Somehow long again
Tinged
For a while
With reality

Now
Gallop ahead
Filled and frothing
Towards
Mountains
Previously ignored

Though visible
To the naked I
Through
Cloud rain mist
Summer haze
The days
Somehow long again

Sunday

The Sunday sunset
belongs if to anyone
to you woman
as a friend

Across the afternoon
more languid than
the Murrumbidgee
at hot summer's end

Than Canberra's winters
dirt roads into wine
your body is trees
in a wind without bend

Termination Overrun

Out of shockwaves you danced
and your vengeance was all but discreet

Like a foundry that blanched
your hammer so damnably sweet

I take it you are destroying them all
wrath and futility simply balance the fall

The Desert

Brooding
Swallowing
Each sound
Each movement
Each desert

Endless thoughts
Sunk in the bores
Of our minds.

The Hand of the Carver

Like set pieces
on a smooth as if
brown board the
hand of the Carver
had been unwilling to end

Pelicans in thousands
take positions
on the long,
brown board of the
Darling River in spring

Waiting to make their moves
slicing quickly the surface
with pink bills
in the early morning
sharpness

Gulleting breakfast
before other set pieces
are moved
to paddle closer
courteously,

To the action.

Cracking Plaster

Mesmerised by cracking plaster
Solitude without the laughter
Floods of white to hide the fright
The chooks are roosting on the rafter

Patchwork quilts and sugar dolls
Stars that leave the sky at night
Water fowl call through the swamp
Sparrows that can learn to write

Just the edge of one idea
Or a tiny spark of reason
Colours in the lives we fear
And changes every season

Junk lies all around the yard
Years of toil still make it hard
Knowing looks and gloomy books
Feed all souls on tarot cards

So awake that eyes are somewhere
Not within their human sockets
Taken on the form of wanderers
Geared right up with metal sprockets

Tingling art form bones and flesh
Dressed in nothing quite like tissue
Sickly grey so what comes next
Drip tears of blood for the next issue.

Young Tom

Thick grass languishing in raindrops
soaks his shoes
before he even gets to the fence

He pushes down on the third barbed strand
flicks his body through
into the lower paddock

He can see over the last rise
that the creek's up
after the rain

But not enough to preclude a swim
which is his aim
of course

And to see Wendy
if she has come down
by the hill road

Branches and the occasional piece of rubbish
swirl passed
as he watches from the bank

She is not at the usual spot
she knew
if the creek was in semi-flood to go upstream
to the big meander
it was always calmer there

Young Tom slides down the bank
kicks his way to the water's edge
dry sand under the surface makes his track easy to spot

'Down at the bend'
he traces in the sand and dry words emerge
if Wendy comes down from the hill road

She will have to come past here
he thinks
and she will see his message

He bends
collects a long-dead branch
not to measure depth
he knows that already

From regular landmarks
just picks it up
hurls later into the middle of the creek

Catches in the swirl
snags three miles
downstream

He expects to see Wendy waiting
not for any particular reason
no prearrangement

Just trying to
think her there
it has happened before

That she arrives at exactly the same time he does
when he thinks her there
not this time

She is not at the creek
in the normal spot
and she is not up at the big meander

As Young Tom discovers
when he momentarily
tops the rise.

Too Many Fruit Shops

There was mostly bush
once
not so long ago
even as far as forty years
an old dirt road snaked through town
old Ruby kept a fruit shop
right next to the hotel
Nick the Greek kept a fruit shop
right next to the solitude of the bush
Nick kept a shottie
close beside him when he went to sleep at night
Ruby kept a flask of gin close beside her
when she went to sleep
there's a supermarket there now
where Nick had his fruit shop
Ruby's became a Chinese takeaway
Nick and Ruby always had something in common
too many fruit shops
now they're both gone
maybe they went back to the bush.

Torment

Drift
Not unlike snow on a stormy night
Between the spaces in a life
Or the chute
Of an avalanche

Arrest remains
Out of the question

Drift
Without anchor without wind
And the wedge must come to
Its thin end
If only to equalise
What pressure there is

Alternatives remain
Illusions

Spin
Until no cover hides no break decoys
Then only with that memory
Can a start
Become the benchmark to renew

Valence remains
In the equation

At times
To yield can mean the difference
Between
Significance or end

Saving face
Remains ambition

Days to Play

Our packs are always primed to go
Never let the pace be slow
Plenty of mountains many more ways
To climb up high on winter days

There really is no urge to leave
Can we rest awhile and breath
The nights are long, cool and sleek
Camped down by Rodriguez' creek

Tramp across the Engineer's by-way
Rest beside the Western Highway
Can we stop and talk a while
Or float by with your casual smile

Now we walk on down a road
Lightened thoughts, share the load
Wherever we might come to next
Together we match any test.

Vivus Sectio

(For Patrick White)

With eyelids slowly closing I slip into your mind
a deluge out of time transposed tells me to unwind

No hash no cash no aeroplane ticket
I lie awake as if in a thicket
of blackberries

Figuring in an effort to grab me on every side
tearing me skin from limb

And flesh that gently laps
the tide of waves

As they break kindly on a sandy shore
feet dripping softly opening every pore

I read somewhere of reality
hating every word

I dream I am a sea elephant
and come breathing on the town

I dream of lovely ladies
in white uniform like a nurse

I wake up turning softly
and at once begin to curse

Such derisive tones about me
casting shadows on the ground

I lash out ever feeble
who is really like the clown

So I think no more of sorrow
or the pain I'll feel tomorrow

Like a listless dying leaf from a tree
that barely quivers
as it flicks and bares its teeth

Run off towards the mountains
to find solace in the stone

I can see the things I trust trust me
and here I have a home

So take a part of drastic art
and tear it limb from limb

Like everything that's served up
from the bottom of a tin

We find the artist rushing by
in time with nothing else

Only he can see through
format and immortal canvas white

Hear a tune that starts with nothing
just to hurtle through and bite.

When the Flagon Was Finally Empty

There was not much else
To talk about
So everyone who had a home to go to
Did

Besides
It was el cheapo wine anyway

Whites of Their Eyes

Black crows
Soaring
Think we're dying
Look at them all
One each
Hope they've got big
Appetites
Black crows

Windbreak

The grassy lee of rocks
After such high driving
Wind
Etching lines
Squinting eyes
Against powerful beauty

West Wyalong: A Postmodern Impression of the Bush

Ten pubs
a staggering drunk
well before closing
lurches at the
caravan park
along the western highway
almost collected
by a Finemores
on the limit
sustaining the share price

As a fat girl
dispenses
hamburgers
to thin private school
girls.
Ah! The Paragon
in every town
virtuous Greeks
dishing up
sustenance
in place of philosophy

As the last of the
tour buses dispense
late arriving pensioners
outside gaudy motels
displaying large in
letters three feet high
Seniors Cards
some tight lipped and nervous
others raucous after
the adventure of
the Hay Plain
avoiding endangered
Mallee fowl
in the late afternoon light
as the driver pushes
to make his scheduled
stop in the schedule

While the postmodern
in West Wyalong is
displayed evidently
as a mobile phone
creates the need for its owner
to be heard
a block away
at the next pub.

City Dream Country Nightmare

You're part of the city you can't change your ways
Walk on the quay side silence of days
Asphalt and pigeons sunglasses smiling
Drunk on the benches nothing for days

You're part of the rotating clockwork dilemma
Spending you life in a circular way
Living believing that God's in the building
Sitting and watching day after day

You're part of the city the sun shines behind you
Walk on the quayside avoid the wet dew
Concrete and windows faces consoling
Lie in the shadows take all your days

You're part of the city you can't change your ways
You're part of the city the sun shines behind you
Walk on the quay side avoid the wet dew
Walk on the quay side the silence is you

Another Sunrise

I haven't seen the sunrise
In the past few days
Been sleeping late
Sleeping off the haze

Been walking in the evening
Near the mountain side
Get so tired sometimes
Just need a place to hide

You don't need excuses
More like a lot of space
Nothing's hard to handle
If you meet it face to face

Hide behind a mountain
It might crumble like a stone
Swim across the ocean
You might always be alone

I've seen a lot of sunsets
In the past few days
Waiting for the moon to rise
A thousand silent ways

Arc of an Angel

The limits of my transition here
Are to a bird out on an ocean
Without a wave
Without a wing
No consequence of motion

Not unlike a mountain
Without snow
Without a climber
Beginning where the sea unfolds
Her beauty to a diver

Axeman's Interior Monologue

I

Abbreviated, the Axeman swings
As if by spirit alone within his own arc
Shoulder to shoulder
An even-handed extension of
The ineluctable modality of the visible.
Less arbitrary, less reductive than
Counsel without cause, breath without pause
Wallaby without claws, history without maws
Sing me your weekly hourly song
I need it like a toe needs a thong
A hippy a bong, a reposed tropical storm, a sarong.

II

Seven blows before a sliver of gum
Wired like the jaw of age
Splits from the keg of the trunk
Drunken
Rolling about as if losing a limb
Is fodder for mirth
Girth gives way to warm the cold nights of winter
Waiting
Next off the woodpile rank
Waved down
With a rush of midnight air.

III

Watch the blistering pace
Until no time passes
With blistering palms
Glasses
Raised in sweat
Within moments
Nothing is as it appears.
This afternoon
As the setting sun
Blots the rust on the unsharpened blade
A cause for rumblings
Behind certain headstones

IV

Bites
The blade
Smooths
The shaft
Away jumps the
Length of time
Counterbalanced
With merely a millimetre embedded

VI

Here's a quick sum.
How much wood can you chuck
In the back of a one tonne ute
before it's sprung?
You can drive the ute and I can drive the ag bike
Up the back to win some of that
Old yellowbox you
Saw and heartset
Jumped and jumped with reminders

VII

And how keenly the blade
Slices through the stags head
Red searing and silver as the tin, empty,
Cleaves in two.

VIII

What happens when you
take no spare handle?
Onto the real live Plumb
Hiding under the old maize sack
Peekaboo, just you and me
We're the ones going to do the work.

IV

Shirtless you chop between beers
As the woodpile growing, seeking
A comparative advantage
Over the can pile.
Angling up with only the merest grip
Shoulder to handle
As you file down slowly the cheeks
Drink chop write, chop write drink,
Split write split, drink drink split
Load load drink
Drive.
Count nothing. Nothing to count.
To market to market to top the price.

IX

Bung some more bloody draught on the ice
Don't just sit there on a stump
Hoping it will all go away
Tell her what you really think
But for God's sake don't frighten her.
Underneath all that gloss and beauty
Lies an intricate tangle of worth.

Backroad

Your house is empty
Without walking by
He knows
Moss slowly gripping roadside shoulders
Strengthening towards spring
Stretching over bitumen
Is a dead giveaway

The road, Jack
Not as good as a warm bed
Late nights
You all need your madrigals

Somewhere along the dirt
Way, way out
The wheels kept turning
To the tune that you remembered last
Distant past

Leaping over the dingo fence of desire
Built to keep in and out
Apart
When in is no deeper than out
It means
Somewhere along the route
Bitumen turned to dirt
But you failed to notice

Another schooner should see a result
If you take it to its extreme
But right now
You're only halfway there

Dog's Dinner

No matter the occasion
Jeff always says dog's dinner
When he feels satisfied

If he was a dog
Jeff's dinner
Probably wouldn't mean a thing

Dr Wisdom's White Hot Hall of Adrenalin (& the Mean Black Tango)

Hot morning sun
Comes crashing through and splits the night
Drives all your memories
Through a piercing shaft of light

Sun can you find me
Sitting in an ice cream cone
We're all alone

It's seven-thirty and the heat's intense
Scalding the concrete
Searing all the minds at rest

No lack of broadloom
In this lovely hall of mine
Lie on the sofa
But be careful where you spill the wine

Son can you find her
Your mother in an icy dome
She's flying home

It's now nine-thirty and the fires' curse
Sapping your energy
Like a bloodstained nurse

Cold icy rain
Comes flying from the hazy sky
To your hall of wisdom
To bend it like an ugly lie

Do you need a coachman
To show you through this world of sin
It's only tin.

Feathers

Sometimes there is a poem
Other times there is a brush
Now
You are winter
Watch
Forever rush

Take a part of total being
Take it to have
Meaning
Give the words to threshers
Watch
Them gleaning

Find a piece of evolution
Show it form and colour
Hang it from the
Kitchen wall
Watch
Eat supper

Give me just one moment
Trade you
For a word
Then the beauty in reality
Becomes
Feathers to a bird

Dubbo Abattoir

Muzzled dogs scream at each flank
pushing fear further up the chute while
rubber conveyors each leg bind

Slowly you move, eyes calm now
away from the mongrels, breathing more evenly

Until electrified you drop, leaden down the belt
to the waiting bloody slice of the halal butcher

Brown, senseless, dead-eyed himself
evenly parting each throat almost imperceptibly.

Slaughtermen move and move again
carcasses now still bleeding draining life

Stripping skin mechanically away
ripping sixty of you each hour

A tiny role in the packing order.

Shearers split heads neatly in two
while brain packers fill tiny rectangular boxes
for Europe

Cropping under the blazing afternoon sun no more
sweet lamb.

Your still remains in the boning room
Quiescent for forty-eight hours

Down the Celsius scale from twenty to twenty
Before your final journey to table

What were you trying to prove
hanging around on those hooks
your bowels on the floor your skull stripped of skin

I looked into what was left of your eye
And I'm sure you were still thinking
your final decision through

Until the head splitter shearer
Once you went through there I could read nothing
Of what you were trying to convey

You ought to have stayed off the belt in the yard
before the mongrel dogs, before the mongrel butcher

You ought to have cut and run like buggery
With all your mates, but who knew this was the end.

Glassy Mountain Lake

The mountains are white
Now the cloud's lifted
Sun is springing
Down through the leaves

Stop thinking about
All the bad times behind
Now is right to
Head back to the trees

Shimmering acres of glass
Lie below
Glazing an eye right back
To the sun

Stiffening breeze gets up
To blow
Freezing right back from where
It's begun

A fire burning
Through the dead tree branches
Running away from
Or running towards

A glint to yellow
Gold cloud turns to dances
All the same gambles
No simple rewards

Climb up over
A dolerite column
Watch the sun sink
Low in the sky

Lie down in a sleepy
Little hollow
Higher and higher
Almost ready to fly

Illusory Fantasy

Show me extremes
As token exchange
For my dreams

And wonder when reality
Comes knocking on the door
Flying in on legs and tits
Bounce softly off the floor

Give me a chance
For death can be
Surely a dance

But talk of sexuality
Drain every sensory notion
From the actuality
Of loving and devotion

Without the flesh
Within the mind
All spaces mesh

See: understanding of the void
Can lead to greater planning
But where's the beauty in alone
The flesh so all demanding

To create desire
Must act
As a barb on a wire

So: consider fucking as an art
In full contemporary meaning
Then ebb and flow in light and dark
Before the wake of dreaming

Kite Day #1

With grateful acknowledgement to Michael Dransfield

It's a real kite day
Descending
Even death equates
Given ending

And it's still only the
First month of spring

Kite Day #2

On kite days
The leaves blanch
In their
Branch sockets

And tingle the earth
With their mirth

Passing Replay

I'm hanging in that bar again
Not quite sure where you are
I guess I should have known this time
You're into another superstar

Carrying ransom notes between the tables
And passing smiles between your faces
Let me get ninety-nine per cent up this time

It's just another Saturday night
And I'm full tilt out of my head
Looking back across that bar
You're everything that you said

About the hard time and your friends
Don't smile or try to make amends
I couldn't stand to have you in my lines

It's only been a month this one
Plenty more have gone before
I'm fortunate to be so sure
All along you knew the score

I played blind in an empty court
We lost between us and the more
I think about it the simpler I feel

Call me up with a smile and laugh
Sure be good to understand
Maybe you could explain it all
Before I become too bland

I didn't say I love you
You know you don't give a damn
The pace was too hot for me and my song

The same old bar, the same old tune
I don't think we could ever share a room
Without freezing and dying in the heart
Didn't get too far from the start.

Wendy

It's like when
Wendy
walked around the side of the house
for the first time
three years ago
and
the dog jumped on her

Mittagong Morning

Through the trees
A cast off breeze
Brings leaves upon the ground

Fat possums crawl
Inside the wall
And bawl a fearsome sound

An owl in the shed
Prepares for bed
She's fed and awaits nocturne

The dogs all hear
With sensitive ear
A fear of growing dawn

With watchful eyes
The hackles rise
As cries pierce through the morn

Chooks in the yard
Peck out the lard
Still hard in the early dew

Timbers creak
Gutters leak
As sparks streak up the flue

The sun gets high
In the Mittagong sky
While a magpie eats a worm

A sheep is dead
Hung in the shed
Until he's bled and dry

White flowers bloom
With vague perfume
And loom towards the sky

www.ingramcontent.com/pod-product-compliance
Lightning Source LLC
Chambersburg PA
CBHW070917080526
44589CB00013B/1342